Trouble for Jasper

Story by Michèle Dufresne
Illustrations by Sterling Lamet

Contents

PIONEER VALLEY EDUCATIONAL PRESS, INC.

Chapter 1
The Birds

"Go out and play," Mom said
to Jasper and Sweet Face.
"Jasper, you look after
Sweet Face."

Jasper found a spot in the sun
and lay down for a nap.
The birds were
in Mom's bird feeder.
Mom had put some
seeds out and the birds were
happily eating them.
"Cheep, cheep. Cheep, cheep,"
they sang as Jasper went to sleep

3

Suddenly Jasper woke up.
He opened his eyes
and looked around.
What was that noise?
"Squawk, squawk," went the birds.

Jasper saw Sweet Face.
She had a bird feather
in her mouth.

Had Sweet Face eaten a bird?
Sweet Face dropped the feather
in front of Jasper,
as if she were giving him a prize.

Just then the door flew open
and Mom ran out.
"What's wrong with my birds?"
she asked, looking around.
The bird feeder was now
on the ground and seeds
were scattered everywhere.

Up in a tree, the birds
were still loudly squawking.
Mom looked at Jasper
and Sweet Face.
Then she saw the feather
on the ground
in front of Jasper.

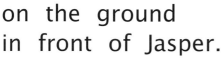

"Jasper! My birds!
Did you hurt
one of my birds?
Bad cat! Oh, what a bad cat!"
Mom scolded.

Jasper was upset.
How could Mom think
he would hurt one of the birds?
He liked the birds.
He liked the birds' songs.

Jasper crept back
to his spot in the sun.
Bad cat? Bad cat?
He was a **GOOD** cat!

Chapter 2
Scruffy the Dog

Mom put the bird feeder
back on its pole
and went into the house.
Jasper went back to sleep.

This time Jasper woke up
to the sound
of a dog barking.
Then he heard
Sweet Face crying,
"Meow, meow!"

"Now what?" thought Jasper.

Jasper looked around.
Where had Sweet Face gone?
He looked over
to the neighbor's yard.
There she was.
He walked over for a closer look.
The neighbor's dog, Scruffy,
was barking and scratching
at a tree. Jasper looked up.
There, on a branch of the tree,
was Sweet Face.
"Well, well," thought Jasper.
"The kitten has learned
how to climb trees!"

He hissed at the dog.
Scruffy's tail went down
and he stopped barking.
Sweet Face climbed down
from the tree and ran home.
Jasper swatted at Scruffy's nose,
and the dog whimpered.

Katie came out of the house.
She ran over to Jasper
and Scruffy.
Scruffy whimpered again.
"Jasper!" said Katie.
She picked him up. "Bad cat!
Don't tease poor Scruffy!"
She carried Jasper back home
and put him down
next to Sweet Face.
"Behave yourself, Jasper.
Try to be a good cat
like Sweet Face," she said.

Chapter 3
Mud

"Mom and Katie have given
Sweet Face the wrong name.
Trouble is a better name
for the little cat," thought Jasper.

One minute Sweet Face
was walking around a big puddle
and the next minute she was in it.
The puddle wasn't deep,
but it was muddy
and the little kitten just couldn't
seem to get out of it.

"Meow! Meow!" cried Sweet Face.
Her little face was black
and all Jasper could see
were her bright eyes.

Jasper hated water.
He hated mud.
"Meow! Meow!" cried the kitten.
"Meow!"

Jasper walked into the puddle.
He picked up the kitten
with his teeth
and dragged her
out of the puddle.
Now he was muddy and wet.

Katie came out of the house.
When she saw Jasper
and Sweet Face, she ran to them.

"Jasper, Sweet Face.
You are all dirty. Oh, Jasper!
What did you
get Sweet Face into?"
asked Katie.

"Mom! Jasper and Sweet Face
are a mess," Katie called
into the house.

Mom came out and looked at
Jasper and Sweet Face.
"Oh, no!" she said.
"They both need a bath!"

Jasper sat in the sink.
He hated mud. He hated water.
And most of all,
he hated the kitten.

Sweet Face was also in the sink.
She gave a little "Meow,"
and looked at him sadly.

OK, he didn't hate her.
But her name should be Trouble!